From
Half-Full
to
Over-
flowing

A Simple Guide to Personal Happiness

PAULA B. LEED

ISBN: 978-0-578-54353-6

Reviews

"While reading Paula Leed's book I recalled an unfortunate childhood memory from a brand new "exponential" perspective. It truly caught me off guard since I've been a practicing psychotherapist for many years! So, you too may find this book to be a game changer! Give it a shot."

--Lorwen C. Nagle, Ph.D., Co-Founder,
Sight and Insight Programs

Paula Leed dissects Happiness thoughtfully, breaking it down to its basic components. Taking each element, she asks us to think about how our childhoods, jobs, friendships and family have shaped our mental and emotional outlook. Perhaps the most compelling reason to read her book is because, as a friend, I know that she talks the talk, and walks the walk.

--Jeanine Collins Malarsky, Author of
Black Raspberries, Maggie's Mirage and Unworthy

"Paula Leed has taken a very complicated and complex issue like Happiness and written about it from a grass roots level. She reminds the reader to enjoy the exploration of what Happiness is, and can be, as she unveils insight after insight. Don't be surprised if you catch yourself saying, I knew that! Enjoy!"

--Joe Sansivero,
Level III Reiki Practitioner

"Wow! What a great book! Paula really nailed it. This thoughtful guide to enjoying a happier life touched and inspired me like few books have. A must read for a life full of best days evaah! "

--David T. Santo,
Founder/Chief Training Officer,
Aerostar Training Services, LLC.

Disclaimer

This book reflects my present opinions and recollections of experiences over time and the effect on me personally. Some names and characters have been changed; some events have been compressed, and some dialogue has been recreated. It is my opinion only that I share. I am not a lawyer, social worker, psychiatrist, psychologist or advisor and this book should not be used as a substitute for the advice of professionals.

.

Dedication

This book is dedicated to my loving parents, Bernie and Sel Leed who instilled in me a zest and love of life which paved my journey to happiness. Thank you from the bottom of my heart... I miss you so much. (ILY)

Table of Contents

The Big Question – Are You Happy?

Are you happy, and if so, how happy are you? How often? If not, why not? Be honest. It's not a test.

__Happiness__

Through most of my life, especially my early years, I heard the expression, "Is your glass half full or half empty?"

I thought about that a lot, and my first response was, "Neither. My glass is OVER-FLOWING!" Hence the title of this book!

From childhood, I pretty much saw the world in that context and I believe my simple way of viewing life can help you feel that way too.

To create happiness, you must be flexible. You must be able to:

- Set goals

- BE REALISTIC

- Set deadlines

- Allow for variables

- Create solutions

- Accept change

- Accept that not all plans work out the way you want

- Applaud success

- See failures as stepping stones to success and celebrate them

- Revel in your accomplishments.

LOVE YOURSELF! My motto is, "Tomorrow may never come; yesterday came and went; your future begins today! Enjoy each day as your BEST DAY EVAAH.!"

<u>Why Choose Happiness?</u>

As crazy as it may sound, this seems like an obvious question. In fact, it is not! Most people do not even think about creating and sustaining happiness in their lives, never mind implementing basic techniques to insure a happier lifestyle.

There are many variables that contribute to making people feel that happiness is just not meant for them. My intention is not to dismiss these unmitigated circumstances, but to embrace them and move forward to dilute their negative impact on life.

One might ask, "What makes you an expert on achieving happiness?"

I don't pretend to be the end all in achieving Nirvana, however, I believe my own experiences in life have taught me the path to being the best I can be. Growing up in a two-parent, middle class, loving family, with one sibling, I already had the basis for a sense of stability - i.e. Luck! My parents were also very hands-on, attentive, gave much guidance, and, were the type of parents we all hoped we would be. Not everything was chocolate and roses, of course, but all were life lessons.

On that note, someone once told me that the things you remember from your life are the things that made a life-changing impact on you – good, bad, or indifferent. Thinking back, I believe this is true. These are the instances that mold who you are, like tiny molecules that build on each other to create the individual that you became and will continue to become in the future.

We usually draw on our own experiences, so let me go back to my childhood again and I will give you an example of what I mean.

I can vividly picture standing in the kitchen next to the stove, watching my mother cook when I was seven years old. I looked up at the open cupboard and saw jars and jars of baby food. I remember asking, "Mommy, why do we have so much baby food? I'm not a baby anymore!" She proceeded to tell me that my father had a sickness that made it hard to eat solid food. In fact, it was the first time I found out my father had severe debilitating rheumatoid arthritis, which changed my world forever. Unbeknownst to me, from that day forward, whether consciously or unconsciously, I became aware and forever protective of my father who would slowly deteriorate physically. He always had a positive attitude about life, explaining that there is always someone worse off than you, no matter what is wrong with you.

With that example in mind, try to recall a moment that sticks in your memory from childhood. Really focus on bringing back details and conversations. If you do this enough, continually returning to the same memory, you may find that you begin to remember more details. Who said what, how you felt at the time, and eventually you may realize how it affected you even at a young age. Fast forward to now and dissect the memory. Think about what effect it had on your future actions and reactions. Would you make changes in how you dealt with these specific situations, especially since you have now "worked through" and learned from this memory?

You don't need to feel obligated to reevaluate your decisions over the years. Just become aware of how you are coping with the past and how the results of this coping process relate to achieving your true happiness. For example, in my instance, I became somewhat of a protector. I felt a sense of responsibility to sometimes be the parent and not the child to both my Mom and Dad as well as others. I'm not saying I felt that at seven years old, but the feeling was buried inside of me and tends to bubble up to the surface when dealing with people. This can be a good characteristic or it can be detrimental. This knowledge gives me the power to choose my behavior and control my actions / reactions. The feeling of happiness and achieving happiness should be warm and fuzzy, not tedious or leaving you with a sense of dread, but ultimately it is a personal choice you alone control.

Let's get back to memories that trigger reactions. Write down everything you think of. Start with an early memory (we will get to ones that are more recent later), to hash over and play out in your mind. This should never be negative. Even negative experiences have positives attached to them regardless of whether or not, you think, "I will never do *that* again," or "*That* taught me a big lesson," or, "My choice of friends will be forever different!" Don't look at any past experience, at this point, as being toxic. No matter how bad it was, it is in the past. You got through it, and it left its growth scars. Some things you had control over, but there were others over which you had none. Life isn't black and white. Never beat yourself up over any past decisions, right or wrong. Keep telling yourself no matter what, it is in the past.

Choices - The Key to Happiness

Choice is the best word in a person's life! We most often (not always) have choices - from simple, inconsequential ones to life changing ones. The number one choice you have is to choose what most closely fits your ability to be happy. So often people do not put enough thought into making choices. Really ask yourself, if I make this choice, will it make me happy? If not, why not? Do I feel pressured? Do I feel I don't *have* a choice? Yes, sometimes choices are out of your hands, but when one makes a choice that makes us smile, endorphins are released. Unfortunately, the realization that happiness is something that we are in control of comes with age and experience.

Death often is the catalyst for this awareness; loss of a child, loss of a parent, or even a pet. It can even be a celebrity, anything that triggers a sense of mortality. Be aware of these triggers and do not dismiss them. Happiness is an emotion that needs nurturing. One must be aware of the feeling every day and make the choice to attain it. Sounds like work? Well, it is, but fun work! Play it in your mind like a game. Does this make me happy? Can I do something to enhance my happiness? Will I be creating unhappiness in another human being if I make this decision? Is it worth it? All are valid questions... But again, the choice is yours!

"Take time to smell the roses." "Always be the turtle not the hare." These old expressions, to this day, hold true. I frequently hear someone say, "I just don't have time." Whether it be taking time to work out, go for a walk, read a book, or sit by yourself at the movies, this "me time" re-energizes you. If reading a book is special for you, go to the library for an hour, force yourself to carve out time and take your pleasure to another level. Do something you don't usually do - something that feels so foreign but natural at the same time. Feel yourself "sink" into the feeling like you are sinking into a cloud. Focus on how it makes you feel... guilty or happy? Maybe both?

Happiness is a Moving Target

To achieve happiness, you must be aware of what happiness means to you. What makes you happy today is not necessarily what will make you happy next year or even tomorrow. It should be peace of mind. A sense of well-being that can range from simple contentment in some people to intense joy in others. It is not only an emotional state but a mental state. Positive feelings are the result of security, comfort, and peace within oneself. It often stems from a sense of clarity, accomplishment or even adulation from colleagues or friends.

Friendship contributes immensely to a feeling of happiness. Having a very small family, I have drawn strength from my friendships. They provide the fuel for my soul: a non-judgmental support system, not necessarily being "yes" friends, but having the trust and confidence to be kind, fair, honest, loving, and supportive. This means being willing to hear truthful opinions and comments while not letting it alter your bond or relationship. On the flip side, to be a great friend in return is another way of achieving personal happiness. Having the ability to be the supporter rather than the supported, allows one to draw strength from positive energy without giving up a part of one's self. That alone creates harmony and is one of the best ways to create personal joy. When we are unselfish, we create a safe environment for another to flourish.

Happiness is contingent upon this complete give and take.

The "Super Glue" of Happiness

Is Relationships

Relationships & Happiness

The satisfaction one can attain from strong emotional bonds with people is magical. Whether it be one deep emotional connection or having twenty people that fill different basic needs, the enriched feeling one gets from healthy communication with other individuals is priceless.

Forming bonds and lifelong friendships is an integral part of being happy. Let's discuss the core of a friendship. What people always notice about my extensive group of friends is their diversity - not only in ethnicity, but in age, finances, looks, background, etc. Most people tend to gravitate toward people like themselves, whether it be regarding wealth, ethnic background, or even attractiveness!

We often fail to realize the pertinent part of a human being is their core values. I believe, core values are what draws me to make a new friend. Not how they look, not how much money they have, not what they do for a living, and so on, but who they are as a human being. In Yiddish, it is called being a mensch. It is considered to be, in my mind, the nicest thing anyone can ever say about a person. A truly good human being has a good character, a good heart, a good soul, and is selfless. I could add traits like: giving, warm, sincere, and genuine to the pot, but you can see where I am going with this!

When I say, "My friends have the general principles and value system that I have," let me clarify even more. This does not mean they have to have the same political views that I have, but, instead, the mutual respect and admiration we have for one another supersedes discord and allows for freedom of expression without judgement. The expression, "You are who your friends are," is one of my favorite expressions. Nice people hang with nice people; shady people hang with the same. Choose your friends wisely and allow for growth spurts as well as plateaus in those friendships. Relish the fact that there are certain friends you may see only once a year or every ten years. When you get together, it's like no time has passed. THAT is a true friend!

<u>What is Happiness to You?</u>

Happiness may seem like an ambiguous term. What is happiness and how will I know if I am happy? We cannot expect to be happy 24/7. If we were, we would have no other emotions! Many people will disagree with me on this, but I am a true believer that a person cannot understand true love if they don't understand hate. People often say that no one should hate. I see it as hot and cold. There is ice and there is boiling water. One extreme to the other and all that is in between... the gray area. I like to know extremes so I can appreciate them more, especially when it comes to happiness.

I don't use the word hate lightly (although one may say "I hate cauliflower" or something of that sort) but more in reference to something that destroyed nature or even humans. It's okay to feel hate. It's okay to have serious likes and dislikes. It's okay to let your mind travel to places that make you think about the world and your place in it. It's even healthy to let your mind wander outside your usual safe zone. Freedom of thought allows you to grow. Growing each and every day makes us the unique individuals that we are. Choosing ways to help us grow in a positive way is the key to attaining happiness.

Volunteering for an organization or a charity that you feel particularly drawn to is one of the best ways to grow in a productive, win/win way. Anyone can write a check, and don't get me wrong, most charities would not be able to exist without monetary contributions. I have a great appreciation for philanthropy; I am just suggesting another way to build your self-esteem that, in turn, will aid in attaining happiness. It's nice putting a dollar in a charity jar at the market, but giving up one's time is the best return on investment.

When you volunteer, the sense of accomplishment is beyond words. The clarity and sense of self that we get from any volunteering is one of the greatest feelings on earth. It takes you down a notch to a place that's almost primitive, out of reality. It makes you grounded. Again, when searching for happiness there are certain words that one should never forget. "Grounded" is a good one! Referring to someone as well-grounded is a huge compliment to anyone. It means well-bal-anced and it doesn't get any better than that.

<u>Pets = Happiness</u>

Okay, so, pets are work. That's a state-ment, not a question! But, as I said earlier, fun work! Pets bring enormous joy and satisfac-tion to your life. If there is any way to make a pet fit in your life - go for it! It doesn't need to be a dog. Fish are soothing, also, and bring a sense of calm to one's life. If owning a pet is not feasible for your lifestyle, consider the op-tion of volunteering at an animal shelter. This is life double dipping, reaping the benefits of volunteering and receiving the rewards a pet brings to your life. Take care of a friend's pet occasionally, obviously not the easiest thing to do, but it allows for the joy of being an ani-mal owner without the full commitment, the trifecta! You reap the benefits, the pet owner reaps the rewards, and most of all - The Pet Wins!

Loss/Tragedy/Failure

All of the above gives us an opportunity to grow! Not that we are looking for or want these challenges to happen, but we are choosing to conquer them and better ourselves in spite of them. Letting a loss or tragedy consume us is the path of least resistance. To be fair, one deserves to immerse oneself in misery and sadness when a loss or tragedy occurs. It is the way our mind and body recoup and regenerate from these events. A reasonable time period for moving on is not an absolute. Each person is different, and a reasonable time period could be a couple months for one person, and a couple years or more for another. The extent and depth of loss may determine this. The unexpected loss of a child is different from the loss of a parent simply because the expectation is there, somewhere in the back of one's mind, that eventually we will lose our parents. On the other hand, the loss of a child is always unexpected and incomprehensible.

Tragedy or anything that is a shock in a negative way to one's life, can create a feeling of helplessness. Being helpless is never a good feeling and can compound itself easily if you allow it to. This is when reflection comes into play and reminds you that you have a choice. You may choose to let these unexpected circumstances control you, or you control them. It is your decision to either hold on to the reasons you feel sad, uneasy, lost, or basically a victim, or release them into the universe. Transform those feelings into "how can I come out of this a better person?" A good, happy, deserving human being resides in each of us. The more you allow yourself to self-diagnose, reflect, and regroup, the happier you will be. Allowing for failure is one of the best gifts you can give yourself.

Failure should be looked at as an opportunity in every situation. Failure always brings with it the challenge to turn that failure around, to improve, to become stronger. Failure is in fact not failing at all! It is a lesson learned; celebrate it! Turn it around! Let it go and rejoice in the fact that next time it will be different. Brush, it off and move on.

Love is a Warm Chocolate Chip Cookie!

<u>What is Love?</u>

Love is putting someone else's happiness before your own. It is not losing your sense of self to make someone happy, but instead having a feeling inside that you can love unconditionally and not give up loving yourself.

Love should be the greatest of all happiness. Loving yourself first and foremost teaches you acceptance. Loving yourself makes you a funnier person, a kinder person, a more empathetic person, all the good traits that in turn make someone love us!

Love feels good; it should come naturally and overshadow all other emotions. We cannot buy love, and we cannot force love.

Most people want to love and be loved; it is natural. It is the feeling that makes everything else seem insignificant. You can search for love and open your heart to sharing yourself with another human being, but usually love comes with maturity. Not age per se, but the realization that love is unconditional, consisting of a sharing of the mind, the warmth of a touch, and a smile that says it all. This establishes, a trust and a bond that hopefully will last through eternity. It is so easy to destroy love by taking it for granted, assuming it will always be there, that it just is, and you never need to nurture it.

Love and Union

So many times I have seen "love in marriage go out the window." It is too easy to forget why we fell in love in the first place. Often it is one partner who gets complacent. Unfortunately, unless that person realizes the consequences of such behavior, it will eventually destroy the once happy union. Often it is too late to save the union because negative feelings harbor making reconnecting and recommitment almost impossible. Every effort to save this union and rekindle the happiness is worth working at, but it cannot be one-sided. The most important aspect of this is to stay for the right reasons. If happiness isn't in this union then there are opportunities out there for another. Learn again from the issues (notice I didn't say mistakes) you had, and fix them for your next go-round. Don't let the same behaviors sabotage another relationship. As my mother used to say, "There is a lid for every jar," or as I always say, "There is an ass for every seat"!

<u>Good Choices</u>

In writing this book I spoke with many people from all walks of life. Everyone was asked, "What constitutes happiness and how do you feel people can achieve happiness?" Hands down, the root to happiness across the board was making good choices. The paths that are laid out before us each and every day are numerous. Haphazard decision-making comes with consequences. Thought needs to go into each path's choices, from the tiniest ones to the gargantuan life-changing ones. Do a quick run through in your mind. Try to get into the practice of making solid choices. Not all will be right, but that goes back to the paragraph on failures! The road to happiness is a bumpy one; an obstacle course that is a challenge. Look at it with open eyes and a clear mind, realizing many times frequently there is not a direct path. With some manipulating and compromise, you will eventually reach the right destination. Most importantly, don't lose your sense of self to make someone else happy.

Happiness - Family - Work & Elephants

Happiness and how it relates to family is a complicated dynamic. There are so many parts and pieces to the word "family." How it affects your happiness quotient is a broad area of discussion. Some people say that family makes them happy. Being around family, finding comfort in family, and nurturing the family is a huge part of their daily happiness. Others confess that family has been at the root of their unhappiness and contributes greatly to their feelings of inadequacy or sadness. Whether it be sibling rivalry, feeling disappointment in your family, or the hundreds of reasons one gets angry or depressed even thinking about family is much too complicated to get into. The bottom line is, like a work situation that is unpleasant, and when change isn't necessarily in the cards, the ability to conquer these feelings of misery is key to your happiness.

Work and family are similar because often our work environment mimics our family life. In many cases, our "work family" is no different from our biological family. It is creating boundaries for those intensely complicated relationships that is the difficult part. Setting up a sustainable environment that won't deplete your positive energy will allow you to grow. Setting up invisible parameters with invisible doors that only you create, open and close allows you to adjust to change. It falls back to the fact that we cannot control other people. We can only monitor and control ourselves. How we act and react to problems, and what part they play in our desire to simulate an environment of contentment (i.e. happi-ness) is a never-ending challenge as well as a moving target.

Selfish or Selfless

The nature of people in general is to be selfish. Self-preservation is as natural as the need to breathe and eat. Some people are less self-absorbed than others, but most have the basic instinct to survive and will do what is necessary to do that.

People who are perceived as selfless often have a need to please and be liked. For them saying "No" is not an option and the need to be liked overrides the need to be happy. In fact, some people assume that being liked is all they need to be happy. Of course, one ends up compromising their principles so much, that in an effort to please others their own unhappiness is compounded. This inevitably becomes a vicious cycle that leads to a "chasing your tail" scenario, never attaining the happiness one so desires and instead going deeper into the proverbial rabbit's hole.

So, your next question is, how do I create barriers and insulate myself from negative work and/or family environments? Well, the answer is somewhat simple. Notice I said "somewhat"! Always take yourself out of the situation and imagine someone else has the problem. This is a good trick in a plethora of scenarios. What advice would you give a colleague or best friend if they relayed this story to you? How would you tell them to adjust their behaviors so that it's more beneficial to them? Take your own advice! Listen to your inner brain and heed your advice. Don't assume it can work for someone else but not for you. Always take the high road. Stand tall and firm, but bend, don't break. Give a little but don't feel bullied into going along with the crowd. Each conversation will be unique, but use common sense. A boss is obviously more difficult to either ignore or go against, but how you speak and get your point across is the key. Learn to expect that quite often, people won't take your side, agree with your philosophy, or even want to attempt to understand your reasoning. This isn't important. It is a short race, not a marathon. Win some; lose some. Move on to the next moment in life, work, or family. As my dear friend taught me, "Eating an elephant can only be done one way, one bite at a time.

The Happiness Burglar

Number One Cause of Unhappiness

Hands down the number one cause of unhappiness is Stress! Whether thoughts revolve around money, family, health, or work, these four things are the catalyst of most stress. Managing these feelings is not simple and changes over time depending on life's circumstances. As one gets older, the desire to be stress-free becomes more intense. When you are young, it is very difficult to alleviate these factors from your life, and managing stress is not a priority. It is not on a young person's radar to focus on stress-related concerns and deal with them seriously. Quite often, having a life impacting illness can change our priorities. The things that cause us stress come to the surface and suddenly we are aware of life and death issues. The smaller things that disturb us become irrelevant. Money woes play a huge part in unhappiness. Do I have enough? Will I have enough? How do I get more? Will I have enough to leave my children? All this and more deplete our happy thoughts. The key is not just to eliminate the cause of stress, which may be impossible, but to find better ways to cope and manage the stress-causing culprits. Don't let a "Happiness Burglar" steal your ability to create joy!

__Sabotaging Your Happiness__

Don't be a martyr. Creating a happier you involves the conscious decision to stop sabotaging your ability to be happy. I listen to people describe their life, and in the back of my mind, I think, no wonder they are miserable! They make life choices that almost guarantee misery when there is no need for it! They most frequently do so because a need to be liked overrides the need to be happy. One could say guilt, but I truly believe the word "guilt" is ultimately used to avoid the admission of needing everyone to like them. The statement: "I can't because I feel guilty," is often followed by other telltale comments that all lead back to the feeling of being unloved if I don't participate in this undesirable activity or situation. The ability to say, "No," is quite often not even in the cards for many people, "No" is not an option for them. If saying "No" is not an option for you, then you must decide if you truly want to find the road to happiness and do what it takes to follow the path to happiness. Or, would you rather stay status quo and nurture your misery. Maybe you don't call it misery, but feeling unhappy is a miserable feeling. It makes you feel bad about yourself subconsciously, which compounds the feelings of dread and a woe-is-me attitude. It creates a feeling of sadness even if you argue that it is not that bad. The truth is, *it is that bad*! Everything I am describing is a catalyst to self-loathing. You may not see it, but sabotaging your road to happiness is another way of saying you don't deserve happiness.

I have spoken to many people who feel there was something in life, perhaps their upbringing, that is sabotaging their happiness. Many, I noticed, have come from a large family and being noticed amongst the other siblings was virtually impossible, a sense they were lost in the crowd. In this case one either learns to do things which get them noticed, good or bad, or they shrink into the woodwork, resolving to let others shine. These feelings, whichever ones you have, are lasting and make it difficult to navigate life any other way than what your past has taught you. Recognize your behavior pattern and try to relate it to your childhood. Breaking out of old habits is not an easy task, but change can happen! Give yourself latitude to experiment with decisions that ordinarily would be simple in relation to saying "yes" to friends, family, coworkers, etc. See what happens when you say "no". Keep in mind, your track record has made it evident that you are generally congenial. Anything contrary to your usual behavior will be met with challenges. Be ready for resistance and have a clear and concise reason and answer why a "yes" decision is not an option this time. Don't back down. Don't be argumentative. Be firm and most important, relay clearly to the shocked recipient of this "no" decision that this is not about them, but about you. Perhaps you are saying "no" because it is time-consuming, a financial burden or maybe it is just because you don't feel like it! Whatever the reason, do not feel guilty for saying "No". Instead, sit back and enjoy your new-found freedom, your extra free time, the new you that knows you surely deserve to be not only in control of your own destiny, but in control of your new ability to be happy. You will come to find that saying "no" to people can be one of the most rewarding experiences and feelings one can have.

Find a Passion

<u>Your Passion?</u>

What all people who are happy have in common is that they have interests, hobbies, or something outside the family unit that they can focus on. When they are either talking about it, doing it, or sharing it, the happiness grows. This is different from saying my children make me happy. First and foremost, your children cannot make you happy most of the time. There are huge ebbs and flows in any family relationship. On the other hand, having a special interest in almost anything, even if the interest is the joy of cultivating your friendships, fires up the happy feelings and creates joy and peace when the rest of your life may seem out of balance. Go out of the box on this one: solicit a friend to join a diet group, join a gym, take an adult class in your community, or sign-up for a healthy cooking class - so many options, so little time! I suggest you choose a person outside of your family circle. The more you go outside the box, the better. You will tend to share thoughts and feelings and get a different per-spective with a non-familial friend.

Your Nirvana -
Finding That Meaningful Place

There is a place I believe one gets to when they are at peace with life. They found their "aha" moment with life, their mojo, their inner love for themselves and their surroundings; an appreciation for what they have achieved and where they are in their lives. A little ecstasy in their life can bring a sense of relief that they have found this incredible place. We must be very attuned to our feelings, almost being a mind reader, but, for our own mind and be able to recognize what got us to this place. What makes them tick? What brings them joy? What *removes* joy from their life once they get to this place? You need to continually recognize the experiences and feelings that bring about all these emotions. For example, if you are in a situation that promotes angst, be aware of it. Even if it is not possible to remove yourself from the situation, put yourself in a mindset that speaks to you. Talk to yourself and note that if you are not able to remove yourself from this event, let the situation play out and remove yourself subliminally and play along until it is over. It is a game, yes, but if you have no options, make the best of it. Remind yourself that not all conversations and situations are perfect. Your lack of choice (something you rarely hear me say) becomes a choice. Choosing to block out negativity from this event forces you to take a different approach and make a different choice.

This is a common scenario and will come up often, but "playing along" to the best of your ability until it is over, is often the best way to cope with unpleasant situations. Take again, a work meeting. Yes, you need to take part and not only take an interest and express opinions but share your solutions. But you may feel like you are either not being heard or not taken seriously. Perhaps "know-it-alls" are monopolizing the meeting, raising their voices louder to make themselves appear more knowledgeable, and therefore, more important. A sense of insecurity is often the reason for this behavior, but nonetheless be conscious of these conversations. Remember, this can also take place in a marital atmosphere, group atmosphere, child's school conference, or athletic settings. Basically, loud-mouths are everywhere and make themselves known. These people act like they are listening, but truth be told, they only hear themselves talk, and have no use for anyone else's opinion no matter how impressive or creative it may be. Listen attentively and then state your thoughts in a firm but non-threatening manner. Tell them you heard them clearly but would like to suggest another option. If you continually feel your words are falling on deaf ears, sometimes it is a sign to move on. When that is not an option, then reset your mind, and agree to disagree and not fight the establishment. Don't fight a lost cause unless you have enough to gain. Put your energy somewhere else. Take the high road. Being smart does not mean being a smart-ass. It means knowing when to move forward and knowing when to stop and re-group. It isn't compromising you or anything of the sort; if anything, it is creating a smarter you. Use your head to determine when you are winning and when it is time to walk away. When you pull back and let others show their insecurities you prove your strength.

Achieving happiness does not mean you don't get frustrated or angry; it means that you have learned how to deal with things, good or bad. You like how you see the world and you like how you cope with people, things, and everything in between. You can laugh and are happy with the way you choose to communicate with others. You like you! It doesn't get better than that!

Thanksgiving -The Best Day Evaah!

All holidays represent something that people celebrate, give gifts, mourn, or remember religious stories or events. Thanksgiving is a day in which all people can rejoice in whatever they themselves feel thankful for: no gift giving, no expectations, just taking time to feel good about something! It is most often family getting together. It is not always a joyous occasion but meant to be! It is almost pathetic that one must feel an obligation on this day to find something to feel thankful for. You should be thankful for every day. I would like to say from this moment on, you should make a pact with yourself to find at least one thing to be thankful for everyday! From the moment you get up, think about what you can be thankful for. Getting up for example, look at the alternative! If last week or last year was a particularly difficult one, be thankful it's over. Hopefully something was gained by it, whether it be health related, work, family, or anything in-between. You are now into the next day, week or year, so it is yesterday's news. If in fact it is not, and the illness, stress, or anxiety is continuing, make it a point to do something that makes you feel good, even for a little while. I tend to clean out a closet or drawer. It can be so mundane, but if it gives you a sense of accomplishment, it has done its purpose. A feeling of accomplishment is just that; it makes you feel accomplished! This is such a simple concept, yet so satisfying.

It can also be the simple act of picking up the phone and reaching out to someone, perhaps someone you have not spoken to in a long time, letting them know they are on your mind. That can make someone who feels lonely or down feel loved. It is so easy to create happiness and joy in another human being, but so seldom do we take the time to do that - make someone feel remembered, that they do exist, that they are important to you. As always, the inevitable result of that one simple call in turn makes you, the caller, feel gratified. I truly feel endorphins are multiplying in droves when I take the time to remember someone's birthday, or just take time to tell them they are in my thoughts. Don't forget elderly relatives, or parents of friends even. So often young people "don't have time" to acknowledge their parents, never mind their grandparents. Reach out further than that.

Even your own friends, you know the ones that you often get too busy for, can get a "rush" from a quick surprise phone call from "out of the blue". The holidays are obviously important, and I don't want to dismiss them, but keeping in touch should be a regular goal. Consider scheduling a calendar, Mondays are call days, then set up reminders to call one person each Monday just to say "Hi." Reconnecting doesn't have to be a struggle and, in this case, shouldn't be. Saying "Hi" is way easier than calling to make plans. It's a different kind of call, a feel-good call - a call that is meant to make the recipient feel good and make you feel even better! Go ahead, pick up that phone and dial.

<u>Slooooooow Down!</u>

Feel More Joy

One of the biggest hindrances to creating long-term happiness is the fast pace of life. Whenever I intentionally slow my life down, I feel joy more. It's like eating at half the pace. When you eat a piece of fruit or candy or steak slower, you can enjoy the taste so much more! As much as you want to multitask while you are eating, try to slow it down. Really taste and enjoy what you are eating. It's the same with life. Everything is hurry, hurry, hurry, pick up the pace, or do it faster. Let me go back to, "Stop and smell the roses." You don't need to stop, just slow it down. "Haste makes waste" is a good old proverb. Most events are more enjoyable when you can taste, feel, or smell them.

Take the in-between, extra time to remember why you are doing something, and how it will make you feel whether it be during or after it is over. There is nothing more enjoyable than seeing a project completed and knowing you are the one who made it happen. You made the cake, painted the room, cleaned your office, or you finished the book you started or maybe even wrote! Finishing something you started is gratifying. Make a list of some projects you would like to get done this year. Put them in time frames of this week, this month, this year. These are "not written in stone"; they are guidelines and writing them down will make them real and trigger inspirations. You are not being graded, so not following through isn't going to change your life. They are just little goals that when completed, give you joy. Most of all, make a concerted effort to do these things at a slower pace, and "Take time to smell the roses".

<u>Compromise vs. Happiness</u>

These two words don't seem like they should go together. On one hand, compromising oneself would seem to be a barrier to happiness. Let me give an example. A woman I spoke with had, "on her own," lost one hundred pounds. She had been on a steadfast plan by herself and over a year's time, had lost this weight. Fast forward: she is now in a relationship where her partner is somewhat controlling. Her feeling is that no matter how much weight she has lost and how good she feels about herself; she still sees herself as a "fat" person and therefore the "new" confidence she has gained gets smacked down by these negative thoughts. She allows his spoiled,

bratty attitude because she does not feel wor-
thy based on old, and may I say, unwarranted
feelings of not being deserving of a partner
who is willing to compromise. When a person
compromises, it can create resentment if the
other person is not appreciative and respect-
ful of that compromise. I'm not saying you expect an "attaboy" each time you compromise.
When it is always one-sided, unhappiness is
sure to set in.

On the other side, when you compromise and bend for a loved one, friend, or business associate, it will trigger a sense of happiness in you! It feels good to know you made
someone else happier by indulging their desires and making their feelings a priority
above your own. When you feel the compromise is done out of respect and not because of

a "they won't like me anymore" feeling, it strongly contributes to your own sense of happiness and contentment. So, when compromising or deciding if you should compromise, think about not just being a "people pleaser," which can sabotage your own happiness, but the reasons you are willing to compromise. How will this affect your sense of self? Will it make you feel good about yourself? Proud? Hurt? Resentful? Will it make you harbor negative feelings about not only the person you are compromising for, but yourself, slowly chipping away at the confidence you have worked so hard to gain? Make the choice with a clear head and be mindful when you feel you are compromising to the point of compromising your own true happiness.

"Happiness" - Exercises & Practices

Every day it is important to reconnect with yourself. Unlike meditation, this is a different concept. It is taking five minutes to re-evaluate "YOU," and to reaffirm your commitment to being happy; to revel in the feelings of pure joy!

To do this, you must make a commitment to let go of the past. Even if you messed up today or last week instead of last year, you must forgive yourself and move on. Telling yourself that messing up is going to happen occasionally, but recognizing the "faux pas", is the first step on the highway of happiness.

The most important part of all this is re-affirming your decision to not replicate this behavior. This could relate to work, family, friendship, or numerous other parts and pieces of your everyday life. Again, the key is to MOVE ON!!

Happy Begets Happy

Your Mojo Affects My Mojo

Keep in mind, your mojo affects my mojo! What does that mean exactly? Look up mojo in the English dictionary and it says a "spell" or "magic charm." It is an African term meaning a sense of confidence or enthusiasm. It implies a general sense of joy and happiness by living in the moment, something that so few of us actually do. Life is fast paced and flies by even quicker as we get older. By learning how to "live in the moment," we can "get our mojo back"! "Get our groove on"! "Loosen up"! When you "get your mojo back," you gain a new sense of self-confidence and excitement. Who doesn't want to be around someone who exudes that!

The important aspect of having this elated feeling is that it spreads like wildfire and creates mojo in those around you. It is infectious in a good way. Everyone enjoys the aura of happy people. How could you not? It makes them feel happier by osmosis. Who wouldn't want to share with an upbeat person, one who sees the glass overflowing, not just half full? No one likes to be with a "Debbie Downer" or "Danny Downer." A waah-waah attitude is a drag and pulls down those around them.

Think of it this way – if you were picking teams, wouldn't you pick the people to be on your team that would enhance your chances of success? Imagine you are creating the "Happy Team." Wouldn't you want energy around that spurs you on to achieve your goals, complement your desires, and release your best YOU? We all want to feel positive energy around us. Be the "Team Happy", and others will clamor to join your team. GO TEAM!!

<u>Say Whaat???</u>

Our verbiage can lift us to greatness.
That's a tall order! The simple way people
speak can make us feel happy or sad, feel good
about ourselves or bad about ourselves. Often
people don't even realize that just the tone of
their voice can create a lack of self-confidence. Parents do it to their children all the
time. Employers do it to employees. It's not
necessarily the words that are spoken, but the
condescending tone that is so subtle, which
implies failure or disappointment or a sense
of stupidity. Frequently a parent speaks to
two different children, saying the same things
but in differing tones to each child, not even
realizing that the tone is being heard by one
child and taken in a totally different way than

the way their sibling heard it. So, when a child reacts to a parent in a hostile way, it is often the tone of the parent's voice that creates the negative reaction, or vice-versa. The difference is, as an adult, we need to be more conscious of this behavior and use a tone that is not combative.

Some people use this tone all the time in their everyday life and don't hear themselves. They may be mimicking their own parent for example – that's the way their parent always spoke to them. It is a hard habit to break, for sure, but you will be listened to and heard more if a kinder and less threatening tone is used.

<u>Pecking Order</u>

I have heard the statement that my parent's expectations of me were different from my sibling's. Depending on where you fall in the pecking order, whether it be the first born or the "baby" (which you will be forever known as), your parents treat you totally different than your other brothers and sisters. You may be spoiled or forgiven whereas your older brother, for example, is punished for the same behavior. This mixed message is frustrating and causes resentment not only towards your parents, but towards and between other members of your family. You may feel that your parents give conditional love rather than the unconditional love that one expects. The long-term effects of ridicule, condescending verbiage and the act of being unforgiving will have long-term consequences that will impede positive growth and general happiness.

As a parent, you must consciously recognize how you treat individual children and work at treating them all the same. This will not be easy, but it is necessary to invoke long-term mutual respect. One cannot see one child as the "golden child" and dismiss another or others. This too, is a common thread that I hear when discussing family dynamics. Of course, family and the numerous issues that come with the family atmosphere is a book by itself, but all those little dots of everyday life connect to either enhance your road to happiness or block that road. Being mindful of everyday speech, actions, and re-actions is a full-time job as I have said before, but if you truly desire what other truly happy people have, commitment to the practices that create happiness must be adhered to.

Most fascinating is the reaction you will get from the people around you who will notice the "new" you. They will automatically let their guard down and be more receptive to your thoughts and feelings. It will open the conversation for freer dialogue. It will make for more relaxed and enjoyable conversations. Even if you are having a heated discussion or disagreement, a softer and less attacking tone will change the way others listen to you, allowing for more rewarding conversations and, ultimately, more rewarding relationships. Try it! You may like it!

<u>Diet and Happiness</u>

I know this sounds funny, but the bottom line is, a healthier you is a happier you! You may say, "I already have a healthy lifestyle, and I'm not so happy." Well, let's face it, just eating yogurt and apples and running ten miles isn't going to MAKE you happy, but I guarantee eating unhealthy foods and being a couch potato isn't going to add to your sense of joy! In general, a healthier you will always contribute to a happier you. Changing just a few bad "habits" or stepping up your game to add new GOOD habits will make you happier! How simple! Start in the morning with a healthy breakfast. And yes, don't forget breakfast! The food is the energy that starts your day. And like gas in in your car, you can't run on empty! Furthermore, the higher the octane the better your car runs! So, fill your tank with "High Octane" foods like yogurt, fruit, seeds, and nuts. Take out the high fat foods, sugary drinks, and cut back on alcohol.

I'm not saying to remove cheeseburgers and ice cream completely from your diet, but try to be mindful and limit your intake of artery-clogging foods that weigh us down (pun intended). Start focusing on more helpful foods that fuel our day. Take a short walk if your life doesn't include exercise at this moment. Doing short spurts of exercise, not marathons, ten minutes each, five times per day, is better than nothing. If you already enjoy a high-energy lifestyle, ramp it up and add something new to your routine. Do you run? Lift weights? Play a sport? Add a bit of yoga or

Pilates even if time restraints force you to skip one of your usual activities.

Try something new for a change. Treat yourself to a new food or exercise as a "gift" to yourself. I started adding pomegranate seeds to many of my dishes. They are fun to look at (visual stimulation is a good endorphin). They are more fun to eat as they "POP" when you chew them! And they are GOOD for you - a triple whammy! Throw them on top of oatmeal and sprinkle them on yogurt. Make avocado toast and dot them on top! Cut-up star fruit and kiwis - although more work - also are pretty and nutritious additions to a monotonous repertoire of meals. Creativity takes more thought, but the possibilities are endless. If you have children or guests, make a smorgasbord of different, unexpected foods and let everyone create their own master-piece.

<u>Don't Lie to YOU!</u>

<u>Be True to Yourself</u>

To expect happiness in one's life, it is necessary to be true to yourself at all costs. What does that mean exactly, you might ask? Being true to yourself means talking to yourself in a way never done before. Let's say you tell someone you feel a certain way, something like "I want to go there with you." In truth, you do not really want to go with them, yet you end up going anyhow. Don't kid yourself into believing that you really wanted to go. Be 100% honest with YOURSELF! Understand that you may have gone along anyway for a variety of reasons, but know in your heart of hearts that this is not what you really wanted to do.

Why is this so important, you may ask – seeing that you are going to go regardless of how you truly feel inside. It is always important that you realize your true motives and why you do or say things that you really don't mean. There are a million and one reasons we do things that we don't want to do: obligation, guilt, laziness, and that nagging need to please everyone. Knowing why you go against your will is a key to unlocking the giant vault of Happiness. I could give you so many examples of not being true to yourself, but of all the important things in life, knowing your true feelings and being honest with yourself are what I think are the easiest things to learn.

This leads us to the next road to happiness, self-confession. Most individuals do not know what that means, but to simplify the somewhat obvious: DON'T LIE TO YOU! Practice seeing yourself for who you are, not how others see you. Not how you want to be perceived, but who you really are.

Try this fun test of this theory with yourself and then with friends:

First get a big piece of paper and a pen. Then ask yourself, "What is your favorite animal?" Quickly write down all the reasons you love this animal. Don't overthink it, but describe in detail all the reasons.

Next - write down your second favorite animal. Do the same thing and write down all the reasons you love this animal also.

Lastly, pick your third favorite animal (don't worry, there are no more!). Again, write down on the paper all the reasons you are enamored with this animal.

Now take the paper and cross out the kind of animals and just leave the descriptions for #1, #2, and #3. Time to analyze!

#1 - This is how you want other people to perceive you (read the animal description).

#2 - This is how people DO perceive you (read the animal description).

#3 - This is how you really are!

In nine out of ten cases including myself, it hit the nail on the head! This is so much fun to do "one-on-one" and is usually an "eye-opener." Often, we do not see ourselves for who we, actually, are. We are not true to the world and often not to ourselves. Being honest with ourselves about who we really are and what we want to be, allows rays of true Happiness to shine down on us from above.

The "Peter Pan" Theory

Reaching the goal of being happy can be a lifetime of intensive therapy for many people. I am not a therapist. I truly appreciate that life is not simple, and happiness cannot be broken down to a few simple sentences that will be life-changing. My intention is to write a lighthearted, fun-to-read guide to finding your inner self or inner child's "mojo." Isn't that what laughter, joy, and happiness are all about? Create moments that remind us of our carefree childhood days, that were filled with awe and amazement but were slowly taken away as adulthood and maturity crept up on us.

Yes, we are expected to be more responsible as we age, but don't let aging take away the responsibility you owe to your inner child!

Choose to be happy and start by making this day your best day Evaah... Until tomorrow!

<u>Who Is Better than Me?</u>

Becoming Your Own Favorite Person

Becoming your own favorite person in the world is essential as you pursue the road to happiness! To like who you are more than anyone you know takes a great deal of self-reflection. Can you honestly say to yourself, "I like myself better than anyone I have ever met or known including celebrities and people that have a much grander life than myself"? If you can't, don't feel bad because most people can't! But why wouldn't you be able to feel that way and how can you truly learn to love and actually like yourself best? Understand that this is different than saying, "I am perfect." It is instead appreciating the idiosyncrasies and quirks that make up your unique personality. You shouldn't feel that I am encouraging you to "fit in" or bend to conform to society's norms. I am encouraging you to work on feeling "comfortable in your own skin". Figure out how to best fit into the universe being the you that you are without negatively affecting others. Does that make sense? In other words, BE YOU but a YOU that appeals to the vast majority of the humans and creatures out there who create a beautiful world!

Working on the parts of you that you can improve and that will propel you to wonderful self-love is invigorating and an internal game you can play to create inner peace and strength. Liking and Loving yourself, two different perspectives, doesn't mean being conceited or arrogant. It also doesn't mean you feel you are better than anyone else or that you know more than the rest of the people in the world. On the contrary, it simply means that you, yourself, find You, LIKABLE! What is Likeable and how does one become likable to themselves? Your goal should be to become congenial, but not a milquetoast, opinionated but not obnoxious. Always create a safe space for the ones you are communicating with. Aim to create a genuine, forgiving, and trusting platform that good people gravitate towards! Don't you tend to be pulled into a conversation or group atmosphere where people are warm and accepting? Safe environments allow invisible walls to break down and fill the air with Likable spores!

Where do you start and how do you learn to not only love yourself but TRULY like YOU?

The easiest way to pave the trail to self-love and happiness is to write down the traits you DON'T like about yourself. Don't be shy! Be HONEST! As I said before, DON'T LIE TO YOU! No one will see what you wrote, and you are not being graded. This is for your eyes only (unless you choose to share with a trusted friend which may be helpful and could give you more insight).

Take that list and dissect each trait, one by one. You must have a clear visual of what you see could benefit from a modified or full change in your personality. Attacking this list will not be a piece of cake but the benefits outweigh the work involved, so stick to it!

Let's start with an example of what I am talking about. Say you are a procrastinator.

97

That can have negative effects on you and perhaps, but not always, others. You don't follow up with tasks in a timely manner for a multiple of reasons.

The obvious reasons are:

1. Afraid of the consequences

2. It's too time consuming

3. There could be backlash

4. I don't really want to do it anyway

5. It may go away on its own and I will never have to do it

6. I feel pressured from an outside source

There are many other reasons too numerous to mention. We all procrastinate, but procrastination is one of the most annoying habits a person can exhibit. It can be perceived as not caring or lack of interest. Both are negative! Most people that procrastinate do not realize the negative vibes that threaten not only their own happiness but often someone else's. There can be a negative, far-reaching impact on others, believe it or not, because, as strange as it may sound, procrastinating can have long-term consequences.

Not all procrastination affects others. It can be something you ignore because of lack of time or simply the fact that no one will be adversely affected by your delayed actions. But it is important to be aware that whether it affects others or not, this task sits somewhere dormant in the back of your mind and takes up good positive space in your brain! GET RID OF IT! Do that task, that phone call, that annoying something that you most likely will have to do anyway! As I've always said, "Anticipation is always worse than the reality!"

We always feel better when we accomplish a task. Consider this a task that, when done, is an accomplishment no matter how trivial it may seem to be. You will feel like a weight has been lifted off your shoulders. You will feel freer and happier and, in turn, will be on the road to liking yourself more!

Another way to build self-appreciation, i.e. self-love, is to ask what others see in us. We often lose touch with that aspect and are oblivious to others' appreciation. Do you also allow others to see the best in themselves? When others like themselves more when they are around you, you are doing a great service to them. It is a generous gift to see greater joy and happiness in another human being just by being yourself!

Instead of thinking what can I do to like myself more, the key to your own happiness can sometimes be making someone else feel better about themselves by your presence alone. The karma that surrounds you can deliver spurts of joy to a friend or stranger and you may not even know it!

Naturally, people are attracted to individuals who make them feel a certain way. Some have the need for excitement and, therefore, a spontaneous personality is going to be attractive to that person. Others need a sense of security and a calming influence, which requires a more subdued and protective personality to fit that bill. Others lack fun in their lives and need a personality that brings out their own silly or whimsical side. Some people crave the company of an intellectual person who challenges them. Variety makes the world go around, opening the gates for multiple personalities to serve multiple purposes.

Don't box yourself in whether you are the so called 'giver' or 'receiver' in this dynamic.

The need to sometimes be the one who 'feeds' the other person or the one being 'fed' is the circle of give and take that promotes self-appreciation. Focus on how you feel when sharing your inner self. Does it make you feel loved? Do you believe you DESERVE the feeling of being loved? Do you love yourself more when you share your love? What feels good to you usually feels equally as good to others. Doesn't that make sense?

An important factor in all the mumbo jumbo is that no self-appreciation can exist without taking alone time to reflect and revamp your way of thinking about and dealing with people. You need private time to evaluate how you react and what works and doesn't work for you in your eternal quest to self-love.

So, share your love and not only love yourself more but grow to like YOU more and more each day!

A Few Guiding Thoughts
for Happiness

If you want more happiness, do more of the things that make you happy and less of the things that don't.

Take pride and joy in your work.

Don't wait to celebrate success. Not every success is going to be something huge. Celebrate the little wins too.

Lose your inhibitions blocking your happiness. We are raised to act a certain way that may not represent who we are and how we feel. Be yourself, whom you really are and stop worrying about what others think. Who cares?

Your environment is your utopia.

Wear your happiness like a shield of armor; it will deflect and protect you from negativity, frustration, and anger.

The whole universe is drawn to happy, positive people. No one wants to be around an unhappy, negative, miserable person.

The people who truly love you should desire to make you happy and take great joy in your happiness.

This all makes Sense!

To become one with yourself, we are again going back to basics. Take the five days of the week (saving the weekends for the Grand Finale!) and spend a minimum of fifteen minutes a day on the five senses: smell, taste, sound, sight and touch. Challenge yourself to focus on that inner joy that we keep talking about by only allowing these senses to encompass you. Ready to challenge YOU? Here we go!

Monday ----- Smell

Prepare your experiment by laying out a selection of herbs. Close your eyes and breathe in the scent of each herb. Are you tempted to "eat" some of these smells: mint, rosemary, anise, cinnamon or lavender? All titillate the senses and remind us of the simple, natural things in life, teaching us to relax and be mellow if only for a minute. Take eucalyptus or some other oil scent that you enjoy and leave it in the shower, taking a whiff of the oil each day to ground yourself before the day starts.

Surround yourself with the beauty of flowers. Every once in a while, treat yourself to store-bought flowers when you are buying your groceries! Add to the experience by purchasing some for a friend! That would be like a double dip in happiness! Sharing your newfound joy by surprising a loved one or a friend is instantly gratifying and can put a smile on both your faces for the whole day!

Perhaps a certain smell brings back memories. A perfume, a meal cooking on the stove, even the smell of dirt can elicit a memory. Keep in mind not all memories are happy memories, but elicit a response none the less. Reconnecting with the smell (and sights) of everyday occurrences, that are so often overlooked in the fast pace of life, can be incredibly rewarding as well as uplifting. Make an effort to surround yourself with smells, (candles are the low-hanging fruit

BTW!) that make you smile and create an atmosphere of peace and happiness. As I have said before, take the time to smell the Roses - this time Literally!

Tuesday ----- Taste

Today you are going to lay out five delicacies from honey to chocolate, or even pizza if it makes you happy! Focus on how you feel when you really taste something that moves you to ecstasy. Relish (pun intended) the pleasures of taste. It can be eating and enjoying your favorite meal, or trying something out of the ordinary, something exotic like a passion fruit. Even a kiss can be a taste. If so, choose to remember why and how it is so delicious! You simply want to savor the flavors and remember that life is not a marathon!

Wednesday ----- Sound

What sounds surround you in the morning? Family sounds? Pet sounds? The sound of music or television? Ocean waves can be soothing to some and annoying to others. Traffic or moving trains on tracks are all sounds we pretty much don't even pay attention to in our busy lives and are quite easy to block out. Pick the sounds that actually COMFORT you. Morning sounds will most likely be different from evening sounds. If you listen to music, do you notice that you listen to different music on your way to work, as opposed to on your way home, or when you are trying to get energized versus trying to unwind from the day? Of course, you do! You unconsciously are aware that the sound effects of your day manipulate your mood swings.

Take control of your life's goal to be happy by surrounding yourself with the sounds that create positive vibes!

Thursday ----- Sight

This one is interesting because you can sometimes see your best when your eyes are closed! The sense of sight is often so taken for granted. We see beauty each day, but see it with a grain of salt. We all know why we do that and make excuses all the time to ourselves and the people around us. Stop making excuses for yourself. You don't need to look at an object or a scene to appreciate its beauty. We can use the incredible imagination we all have inside us to interject beauty into our lives every day. Just ask a blind person if they are able to SEE and enjoy beauty. I guarantee you they will say, "Yes"!! Like, the saying goes, "Beauty is in the eye of the beholder". You do not need the gift of sight to see beauty in the world.

Friday ----- Touch

Touch is my favorite sense. When one uses the sense of touch so many deep-rooted emotions and feelings can awaken and come to life in earth-shattering ways. Whether touching another human being, a pet, a furry rug, or even an inanimate object, the sense of touch is amazing. Even Eskimos (who kiss with their noses because their environment is so very cold), as I am told, understand that touch doesn't necessarily mean using ones' hands or feet to extract emotion!

Some people don't like to touch or be touched. For these people, I feel sad. By touching, one can share feelings without ever having to say a word. What a lovely gift to be given in life.

Saturday and Sunday - the Weekend!

I promised the "Grand Finale" and here it is! On Saturday and Sunday bring all the fabulous five senses together for at least half an hour and spend this time doing nothing but enjoying your newly remembered sense of smell, sight, taste, hearing and touch. These do not have to be in the traditional sense. Experiment and play! Hearing for a deaf person can simply be sensing a train passing by resting their hand on a trembling table top or feeling the vibrating ground beneath them. For a blind person, sight could be their imagination showing them the breathtaking colorful tulips in Holland or giraffes running in the Serengeti! WOW! What a sight!

<u>Final thoughts...</u>

Happiness is not something you lock up in a box and take out on a whim. It is not meant only for some, but for everyone. Yes, it is DIFFERENT for everyone, but it should be what makes YOU smile and, what makes YOU want the sun to come up Tomorrow!

<u>Acknowledgements</u>

To my dear friend Jeanine Collins Malarsky. How can I ever thank you?? Your expertise is mind-blowing and your willingness to share your knowledge is beyond words! You are a beautiful person as well as an accomplished author. I aspire to one day be equally prolific in the literary world.

To my husband, Richard, who I could say has had to put up with my craziness while I was writing this book, except there WAS no craziness, so he didn't have to put up with anything (LOL)! He spent hours working and reworking the layout of this book when he could have been playing golf! For that sacrifice I am indebted. Thank you for being a part of my world.

To my special group of friends who tease me for the way I talk, laugh at my jokes, and share their secrets, joys and woes with me, while always trusting. I will ALWAYS have your backs. Too many to name, but you all know who you are.

Thank you to the Palm Beach Foundation Mentoring program that encourages and mentors young adults to pursue their dreams in the literary world. A special thanks to Karima Cromer and Raymond Knudsen.

To my readers, I encourage you to feel free to email me at: Mybestdayevaah@gmail.com.
I will reply to every email and welcome your thoughts, suggestions, and stories of joy! Thank you for reading and sharing my book in your own personal pursuit of happiness.

Paula

About the Author

Paula spends her happy time between Palm Beach FL, Rye Beach NH, and Andover MA with her husband Richard and two miniature dachshunds, Peanut and Peewee. She is a successful business owner, jewelry designer, and exciting fashionista. She fosters amazing friendships with so many kind and wonderful people whom she loves, adores and nurtures. Her mission in life is to make each day the best day ever, living life to its fullest and spreading joy and happiness to everyone she meets.

Her motto is, "LOVE YOURSELF! Tomorrow may never come; yesterday came and went; your future begins today!" Share your love: don't just *love* yourself more, grow to like YOU more and more each day. Choose to be happy and start by making this day *your best day evaah* . . . until tomorrow.

Made in the USA
Middletown, DE
20 November 2019